CROWNING FOLLIES

PUNCH

Among the Rulers

Edited by William Hewison

A PUNCH BOOK

Published in association with

GRAFTON BOOKS

A Division of the Collins Publishing Group

Grafton Books
A Division of the Collins Publishing Group
8 Grafton Street, London W1X 3LA

Published by Grafton Books 1988

British Library Cataloguing in Publication Data
Crowning follies: Punch among the rulers.
1. English humorous cartoons – Collections
I. Hewison, William –   II. Punch
741.5'942

ISBN 0-246-13403-8

Printed in Great Britain by William Collins Sons & Co. Ltd, Glasgow

Introduction

I was down there at The Meeting, naturally. In the basement of Grafton's chic little Regency abode in W1. Eventually after much chat about this and that they got to the business of the next cartoon books. I perked up, reached for my Pentel Finepoint. What subjects, what areas, then? We'd already done Motoring, and Television, and Criminals, and Parties, and quite a few other diversities (what, haven't you been collecting the lot?), all hand-picked from the pages of *Punch* and neatly put together in paperback packages.

Someone read from a list of possibles. Sport? Yes, unanimous vote on that one. Schools, students? OK. Everyone's been to school, even cartoonists. Tick that. Family Life? Well, that's pretty broad, plenty of scope there. Should be popular. Yes. Finally, how about Kings? (*Kings!* I groaned, to myself. How on earth was I to find a sufficient number of cartoons about kings, enough to fill 124 pages? After all, for several years hadn't I been huddled in the Art Editor's chair up at Punch Office, scrutinising the offerings sent in by cartoonists from far and wide, and arguing with the Editor about which ones we should accept? Yes, there had been kings, of course, but only occasionally. Usually sitting on thrones and having sharp words with their Fools. But enough to make a book? I visualised myself scouring the bound volumes right back to 1841, issue Number One, and still short on supply.)

So, time for me to heave a damp blanket over the happy discussion. Too narrow a theme, I said, it should be stretched a little wider. To include dictators, pharaohs, junta colonels, leaders like Nero and Napoleon and Genghis Khan. Especially Genghis Khan, because Bill Tidy had produced a real beauty about Genghis, a real classic. OK, they readily replied. Agreed. I must say they are a civilised lot at Grafton.

Now then, here's the curious bit. After a short time spent burrowing away through the back issues it was evident that kings were popping up all over the place – yes, sitting on thrones but also speechifying from balconies, riding around in carriages, going to the play, calling for horses, receiving their come-uppance – all rendered in a great variety of humour and styles of drawing. As far as the *Punch* cartoonists are concerned, the monarchy is not on the way out.

Certainly not as far as one particular cartoonist is concerned: Hector Breeze. His drawings deal with a lot of things but early in his cartooning career he devised a King character – crowned, sashed, buckle-shoed – to which he returns time and time again. Breeze's people have profiles that seem to have melted a little before some blazing fire; his King is no different. He has produced dozens of them so I've had to pick and choose and ration, as I also have had to ration the appearances of Ray Lowry's Adolf Hitler. At one time he manufactured Hitler cartoons as on an assembly line, so sheaves of Nuremberg Rallies arrived by every post. Lowry's humour is surreal, his drawing style peculiarly his own – a very distinctive combination.

So all the jumped-up dictators and boss-men sprinkled among the royalty in the following pages do earn their keep – their encrusted, bemedalled uniforms, flashier than the simple crown and ermine, add a touch of useful vulgarity to an otherwise aristocratic show. There was a moment when I was tempted to include that oversize gorilla climbing up the Empire State Building, but concluded that the presence of King Kong would be stretching the theme just a bit.

William Hewison
March 1988

"I can still say that we're not a true democracy till we get a Northerner in there."

"Power mad – that's what you are!"

"The lowest common denominator –
that's all they ever aim at! What about
me for a change?"

"I still say this game was more dignified before the sponsors moved in."

"That's all I need – a finicky food taster."

"Do Frankie Vaughan, they love that one!"

"So you have no aspirations…"

"…you're not interested in culture…"

"…you never put anything by for a rainy day…"

"...you're reluctant to try
anything new..."

"...There's no doubt
about it, I'm afraid..."

"...You're working class."

"I thought they'd never go."

ELVIS LENIN

BUDDY MARX & THE CRICKETS

JERRY LEE BREZHNEV

"I see our glorious leaders have decided to rewrite rock-and-roll history as well."

"But will anyone salute it?"

"I don't know how we'd manage without these royalty cheques from the BBC."

"This is Mr Vandenheim, my dear. He needs a kingdom and we need the money."

"I've never seen him half so pleased as he is about this sudden French collapse."

"Now scrape."

"Haven't you two met? Catherine of Braganza, Nell Gwynne.
Nell can get us oranges wholesale."

"She's really an International Socialist,
she's resting…"

"When he starts on
the Divine Right of
Kings – watch out."

"I knew it! I knew it! Sooner or later I just knew there'd be a catch!"

*"What a glorious day! Where's
Stefan Ivanovich?"*

*"Stefan! I want to change places like
we used to! You can be King and I ..."*

*…can lead the gay carefree life of a
peasant for a few precious hours.
Where are you, Stefan?"*

*"Be with you in a minute. I'm standing
in for the Queen till half past nine."*

"Deserter, sire."

"I know, I know – follow that star!"

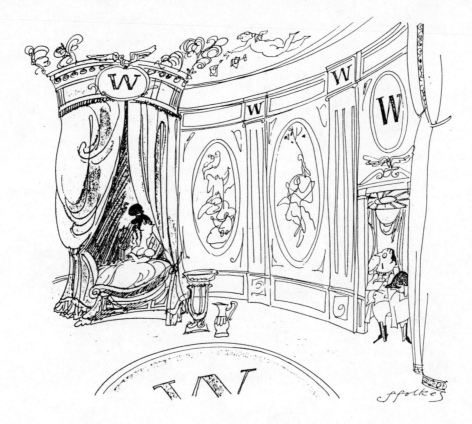

"Who's W?"

"Aw c'mon, Genghis – we need one more to make up a horde!"

"Please be patient! The king is in his counting-house counting out your money."

"Sorry, majesty, the tomb's not in that one. Try again."

*"Gott in Himmel! **Somebody** must have a franc!"*

"That's the deal then. We give you our gold and you give us something called a Spanish omelette."

"I hope you don't mind, we're rather early."

"Hold it! There's been a coup!"

"Where's the fresh-faced youth whose noble features, so full of hope and promise, once adorned the coronation mugs?"

"We'd better get a move on, Sire – the band is up to the bit with the cannons in it."

*"Enough of the civilities.
Have them stewed."*

"There's an idea there somewhere, but it still looks too down-market."

"I have gathered you here today to tell you of
my exciting plans for enlarging the palace,
to include a heated pool, squash courts
and a home-entertainment centre."

"He's been deposed."

"You can't go through life thinking royal weddings are a pain in the neck."

"I'm sorry, your Majesty – the show folded yesterday."

"Damn! There goes my No-Claim Bonus."

"I said…Deformed! Unfinished. Sent before my time…into this breathing world scarce half made up. I never mentioned a word about a rise."

"Well, we ought to take them something."

"*The decisive battle will be fought here ... and it's a good name for a house.*"

"I gather the Queen's taking up jogging."

"I'd like a better life for my children and their children, but if I can't get that, I'll settle for a better life for myself."

"Granted he's barbaric, but his sense of humour is surprisingly sophisticated."

*"Well, I think it was rather nice of that
Japanese tourist to give you a tip."*

*"I make it fifty thousand. Of that, five went on entertaining,
six on palace maintenance, ten on prisons, and fifteen on the army.
The rest went on bread and honey."*

"We who are about to
die salute you…
you fat slob!"

*"I've been king and I've been prince
and believe me, king is better."*

*"For sale. Twenty thousand German helmets never been used.
Ideal for parties, house plants or motor-cycle gangs."*

"Actually, sir, she's out – she leaves the flag up to fool the burglars."

"Mordred's offered him a chat show."

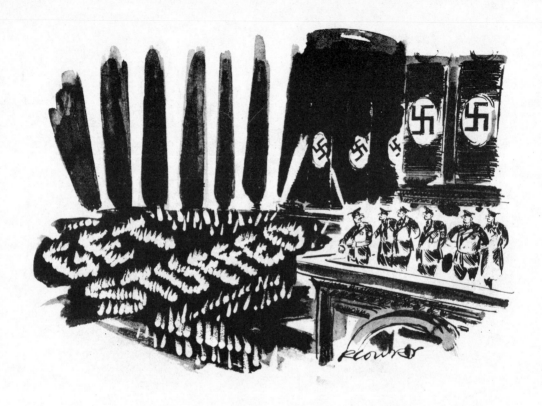

"We've got to do something about these dissident elements infiltrating the torchlight processions!"

"Excellency! The Moderates have seized the radio station!
They're playing études by Chopin!"

"As a footnote to history, I want
it known that Angelica has been one hell
of a good concubine."

"The neutron anti-personnel grenade, General – it
kills enemy troops, without ruining their uniforms."

"Ah, yes, and a question from the back there..."

"I always understood they just shuffled around being mistaken for one of the gardeners."

"It's King Lear all right but who's that with him?"

"*Let them revolt. Two can play at that game.*"

"The Queen and I are rather disappointed with George."

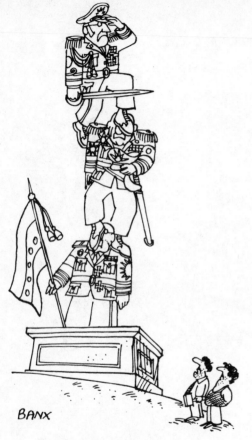

BANX

*"I don't think I could take another
coup d'état."*

*"And don't forget, the King only means it as a modification
in your planned rate of growth."*

"You beggars are all the same – all you ever think about is money."

"To be honest, Your Majesty, we were expecting you to attract a much larger crowd."

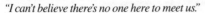

"I can't believe there's no one here to meet us."

"We don't know whether to name him James, the Beneficent; James, the Munificent; James, the Magnificent or Jimmy, the A1, world-class, Top-of-the-Line, Numero Uno."

*"We've settled with the pipe makers and bowl fillers, Sire.
But the fiddlers three are still on strike."*

"Surely you jest?"

"He's either a nut or a very fast draw."

"Sir, the Irish Ambassador wishes to present his credentials."

"Get out and arrest a few dozen
political prisoners in case we have to
ransom an ambassador."

"This is one of those things you think happen only to other people."

*"It's not going to be easy – I mean, everybody
wants to get on the Parkinson show!"*

*"If I had half a chance, I'd swop with my meanest
subject … Paul Getty for instance."*

"This is where I miss the corgis."

"A horse! H-O-R-S-E, horse!!"

"Signify by cheering, all
those in favour of 'tyranny
with a human face'."

*"Given different circumstances he could really
have made something of his life."*

*"Of course, **he'll** never admit it's a U-Turn."*

"So how did the Peasants' Revolt make out?"

"Just remember you're talking to the keystone of the whole edifice of power and privilege without which…!"

"Know what I miss? Getting ideas above my station."

"Personally, I should be terrified going into battle behind
someone who thought he was Napoleon."

*"Great news! Your Majesty – the attempted
revolution has been crushed!"*

"But what's happened to his soaring political ambition? – all he wants to do now is invade Toytown!"

"It all started when I decided to marry a commoner."

"Genghis has come up with this great idea. Kill everyone on sight."

"It's a fantastic diet, sire. The food-taster's lost 15 lbs."

"Gentlemen, we may be Number Two but we try harder."

"Would you mind, Your Majesty … It's not for me, you understand … my daughter …"

*"Take no notice. He's been going on about getting
a few of the lads together to invade Russia for as long
as I can remember!"*

*"This year, of course, we achieved the first successful sack of Rome.
Next year we confidently look forward to the sack of Florence and
Milan, and, if there's time, the rape of Sicily."*

HEATH

"Two loaves... five fishes...
five thousand people..."

"I'm told there was some sort of mix-up."

"Well, including me that's sixty-two beers and a packet of pork scratchings."

"His majesty would like a word with you."

"I'm not some minor Ruritanian princeling, you know!"

"Now let's see – who don't you know?"

"I've had another purge of the armed forces."

"You'd be surprised how often it comes in handy."

"Sir Gawain said he was sorry he had slain the woman. Sir Bors then proposed a resolution opposing the slaying of women, which was passed. A very large knight rode in and challenged the entire company; this was tabled for a twelvemonth. There being no further business, we adjourned."

"I've a good mind to cause consternation among my bodyguards by not diving off unexpectedly into the crowd."

*"I bet **he** got broken pavements mended!"*

"That's six choc ices, two tubs and a drink on a stick up here – and be quick about it, dummkopf!"

"Merlin would like a word
with you, Sire."

"Don't worry about it, dear. Your Father's
just reliving his youth."

"He hates to delegate."

"Dammit! If they were anyone else we could just walk straight to the front!"

"In fulfilment of my promise …

…the time has now come …

…for me to hand over to civilian rule!"

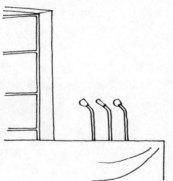

*"I know, why don't **we** throw a bomb at **them!**"*

"*My moves are limited, you know.*"

"I think these phone-in Nuremburg rallies are going to be the death of live entertainment as we know it!"

"He's waiting for a poor man to come in sight."

"You're right. It isn't a blue-headed wagtail."

"You know what I regret? Never having
met anyone on the way up."

"To tell you the truth, I really wanted to be the Dirty Rascal."

"Napoleon Bonaparte on the hot line, Your Grace."

"Gosh, I'm so corrupt, and you're really
swell to take it the way you do."

"Terrible news, General —
the rebels have seized the
military outfitters!"

"It's a delegation, sir. One hundred and fifty million signatures saying what a good job you're doing."

"He's never learned to delegate responsibility."

"He's a talent scout for Attila the Hun."

"You can take the Prince out of the frog, but you can't take the frog out of the Prince!"

*"He's utterly convinced that he's being exiled to St. **Helens**, poor devil!"*

"It's the singing telegram from the Queen, Miss Petheridge."

"*There comes a time in the affairs of men when you can get away with absolutely anything.*"

"He's a born leader."

"It's the Royal physician, Ma'am, and would you slip your things off."

"Your Majesty, this is the Royal Command Performance. You plant the tree tomorrow!"

"From Monday we're slotting you in at breakfast."

"Alternative comedy? You call an exploding pig's bladder alternative comedy?"

"Whenever I need a little boost I dial 'National Anthem'."

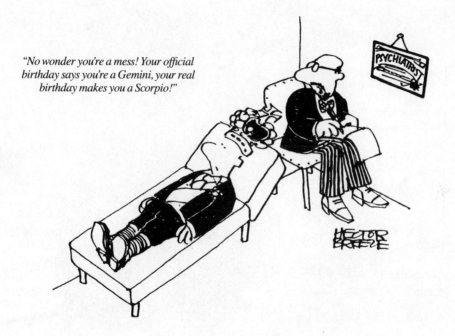

"No wonder you're a mess! Your official birthday says you're a Gemini, your real birthday makes you a Scorpio!"

"It's the only exercise he gets."

"…And, therefore, since an undue percentage of current history is being made by white European males, Mon Général, we feel you should give some of the other groups a chance."

"Yes, but what do you do for a living?"

"Trust old Johnson to over-react."

"It's always the same. You think you have a job for life – then they die laughing!"

"I said the joke's on you, but let it pass."

*"I've sometimes wondered
whether we couldn't perhaps be a
little less exemplary."*

*"If your friend's not here in five minutes I'm afraid
we might have to carry on without him!"*

"Call that boiling?"

"Lighthearted! Skittish! As rumbustious
a little poison as I've ever tasted…"

"I've got a waiting room full of patients out there! What would happen if they all wanted bulletins issued?"